Miles
Kelly

First published in 2005 by Miles Kelly Publishing Ltd
Harding's Barn, Bardfield End Green, Thaxted, Essex, CM6 3PX, UK

Copyright © Miles Kelly Publishing Ltd 2005

© 2012 Discovery Communications, LLC. Animal Planet and logo are trademarks of
Discovery Communications, LLC, used under license.
All rights reserved. www.animalplanet.co.uk

This edition printed in 2012

2 4 6 8 10 9 7 5 3 1

Publishing Director Belinda Gallagher
Creative Director Jo Cowan
Project Manager Lisa Clayden
Edition Editor Amanda Askew
Cover Designer Kayleigh Allen
Designer Tom Slemmings
Reprographics Stephan Davis
Production Manager Elizabeth Collins

British Library Cataloguing-in-Publication Data
A catalogue record for this book is available from the British Library

ISBN 978-1-84810-851-6

Printed in China

COVER Rich Carey/Shutterstock; 3b Jim Agronick/Shutterstock
All other images are from the MKP archives

www.mileskelly.net
info@mileskelly.net

www.factsforprojects.com

INTRODUCTION

Sharks are a fierce and fascinating type of fish. They are brilliant hunters and most have sharp teeth, keen eyesight and an excellent sense of smell. They can usually swim very quickly because of their streamlined shape.

Lots of people are scared of being bitten or even eaten by a shark, but attacks on humans are actually very rare. In fact, sharks have more reason to fear us – some species are endangered because so many are killed by fishermen.

With this great sticker book you can learn all about sharks and amaze your friends with amazing fun facts!

Mini stickers!

What is a filter feeder? How long can the whale shark grow? Which shark has spikes all over its body? Use your mini stickers to find out about the lives of extraordinary and fierce sharks and their relatives.

Extraordinary sharks – weird and wonderful sharks
How sharks live – how and where sharks live
Shark relatives – these are closely related to sharks
Fierce sharks – the biggest and scariest members of the shark family

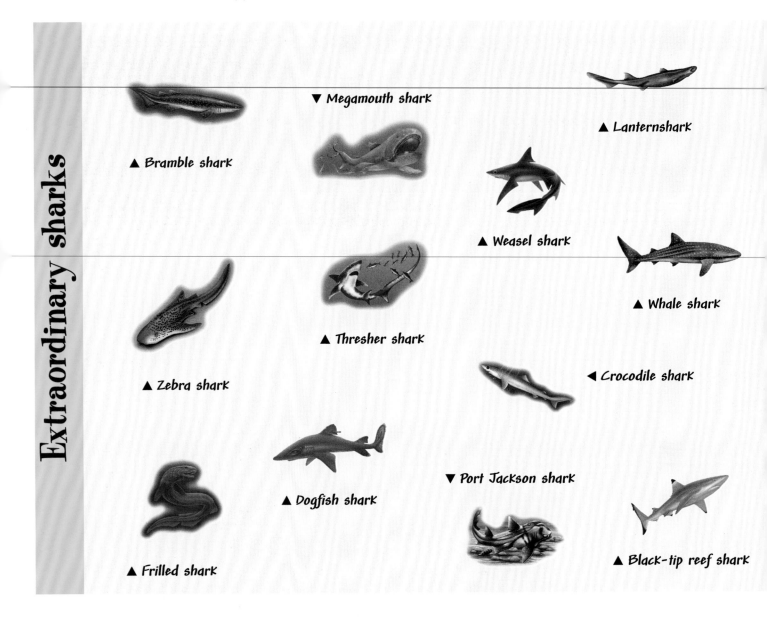

Extraordinary sharks

▲ Bramble shark

▼ Megamouth shark

▲ Lanternshark

▲ Weasel shark

▲ Whale shark

▲ Zebra shark

▲ Thresher shark

◄ Crocodile shark

▲ Dogfish shark

▼ Port Jackson shark

▲ Frilled shark

▲ Black-tip reef shark

How sharks live

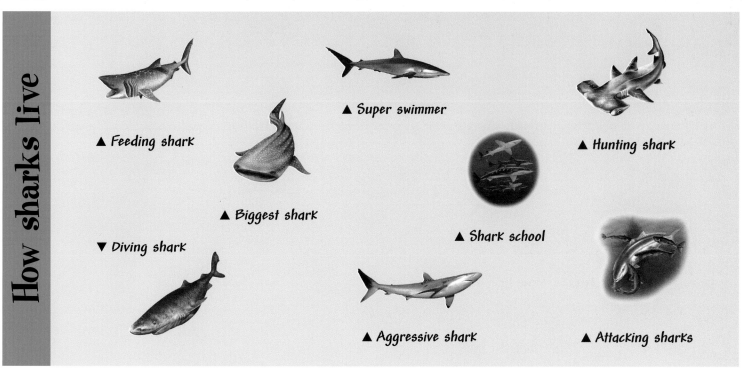

▲ Feeding shark

▲ Super swimmer

▲ Biggest shark

▲ Hunting shark

▼ Diving shark

▲ Shark school

▲ Aggressive shark

▲ Attacking sharks

Shark relatives

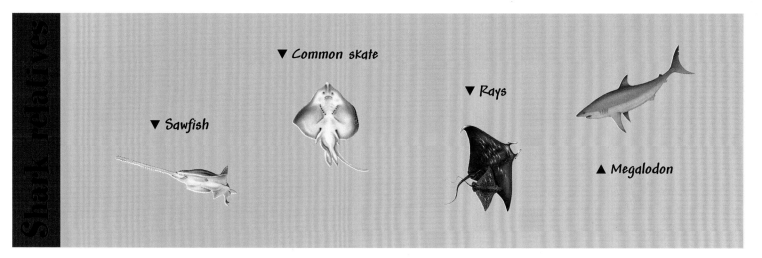

▼ Common skate

▼ Rays

▼ Sawfish

▲ Megalodon

Fierce sharks

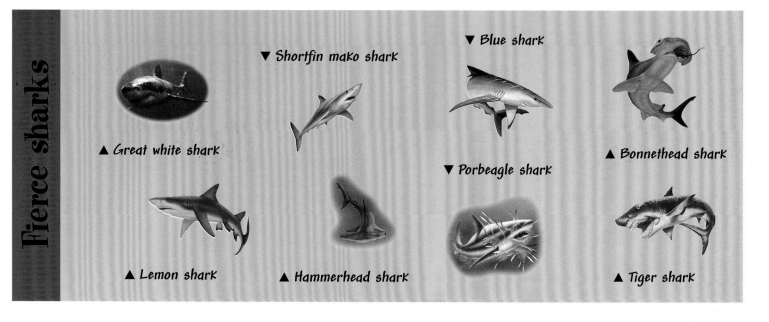

▼ Shortfin mako shark

▼ Blue shark

▲ Great white shark

▲ Bonnethead shark

▼ Porbeagle shark

▲ Lemon shark

▲ Hammerhead shark

▼ Tiger shark

All kinds of sharks

◄ Bonnethead shark
Fishermen have to be careful if they grab a bonnethead by the tail, as it can reach up and bite their hand

◄ Frilled shark
This shark is often mistaken for an eel or a sea snake because of its snakelike appearance

▼ Bramble shark
A shark that lives in deep water and has large, thornlike spikes all over its body

▼ Lanternshark
Glowing lights on their bodies give these sharks their name

▼ Feeding shark
This basking shark feeds on tiny creatures that live in the water

► Biggest shark
Whale sharks are the biggest sharks and they use their massive mouths to sieve food out of the water

► Megamouth shark
This shark lives up to its name with a mouth about one metre in width!

▲ Sawfish
A sawfish is a type of ray and it gets its name from its long sawlike snout

KEY:

 How sharks live

 Extraordinary sharks

 Shark relatives

Fierce sharks

▼ Crocodile shark
The huge eyes of this shark take up almost half its head!

▲ Super swimmer
Sharks are streamlined so that they can swim quickly and sneak up on their prey

► Pygmy sharks
Some sharks work as a group to attack bigger fish that are sick or injured

◄ Hunting shark
At night, bonnetheads go hunting alone for fish, squid, octopuses, crabs and stingrays

► Port Jackson shark
After laying her eggs, the female Port Jackson shark picks up her egg cases in her mouth and wedges them in a safe place

► Common skate
Skates are like rays and mostly live in deep water – as far as 3000 metres down

◄ Diving shark
Most sharks like shallow or warm seas, but Greenland sharks dive deep in the cold water of the North Atlantic Ocean

◄ Weasel shark
This shark looks like a bite has been taken out of its tail – but this is just its natural shape

A typical shark has several hundred teeth at any one time!

Scales and skin!

A shark's skin is covered by small scales. These are very sharp and pointed – in fact, they are just like tiny teeth. The saw shark also has teeth outside its mouth. These run in a row along each side of its long snout.

The saw shark 'saws' into mud and seaweed to find fish and starfish, and eats them using the teeth in its mouth.

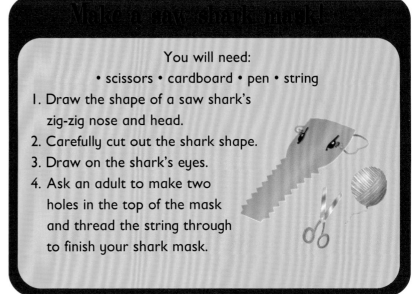

Make a saw shark mask!

You will need:
• scissors • cardboard • pen • string

1. Draw the shape of a saw shark's zig-zig nose and head.
2. Carefully cut out the shark shape.
3. Draw on the shark's eyes.
4. Ask an adult to make two holes in the top of the mask and thread the string through to finish your shark mask.

The snout teeth look like a chainsaw – and they are just as dangerous.

On each side of the snout is a long, bendy feeler – a barbel. It wriggles like a finger in the mud to find food.

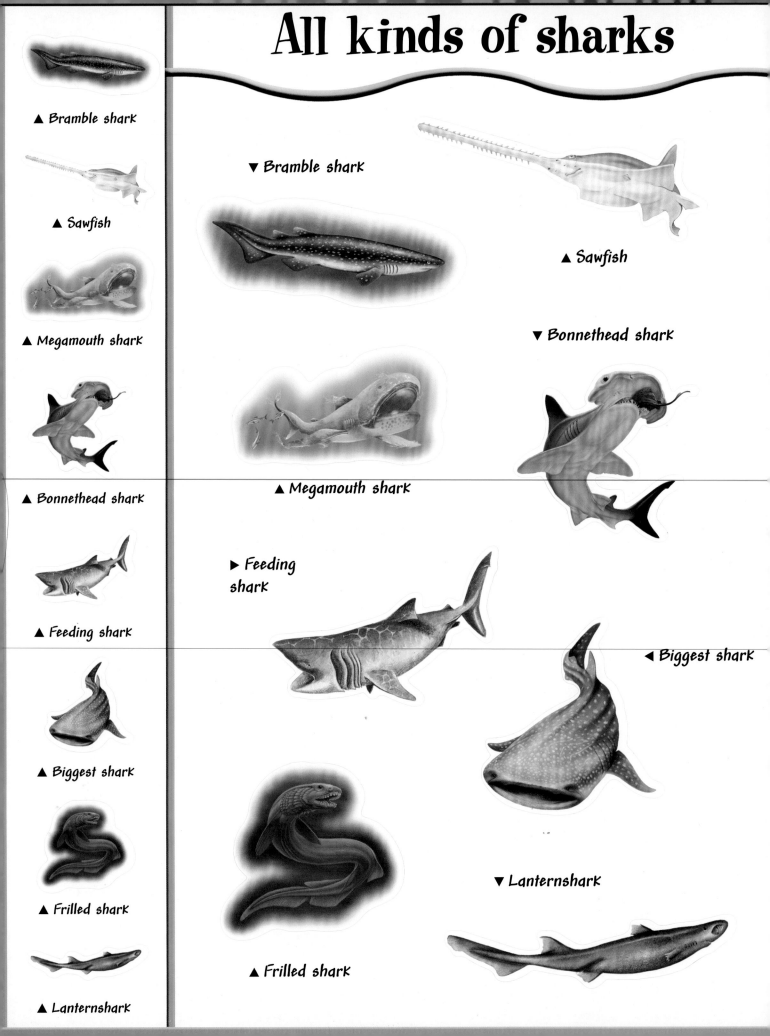

All kinds of sharks

▲ Bramble shark

▲ Sawfish

▲ Megamouth shark

▲ Bonnethead shark

▲ Feeding shark

▲ Biggest shark

▲ Frilled shark

▲ Lanternshark

▼ Bramble shark

▲ Megamouth shark

▶ Feeding shark

▲ Frilled shark

▲ Sawfish

▼ Bonnethead shark

◀ Biggest shark

▼ Lanternshark

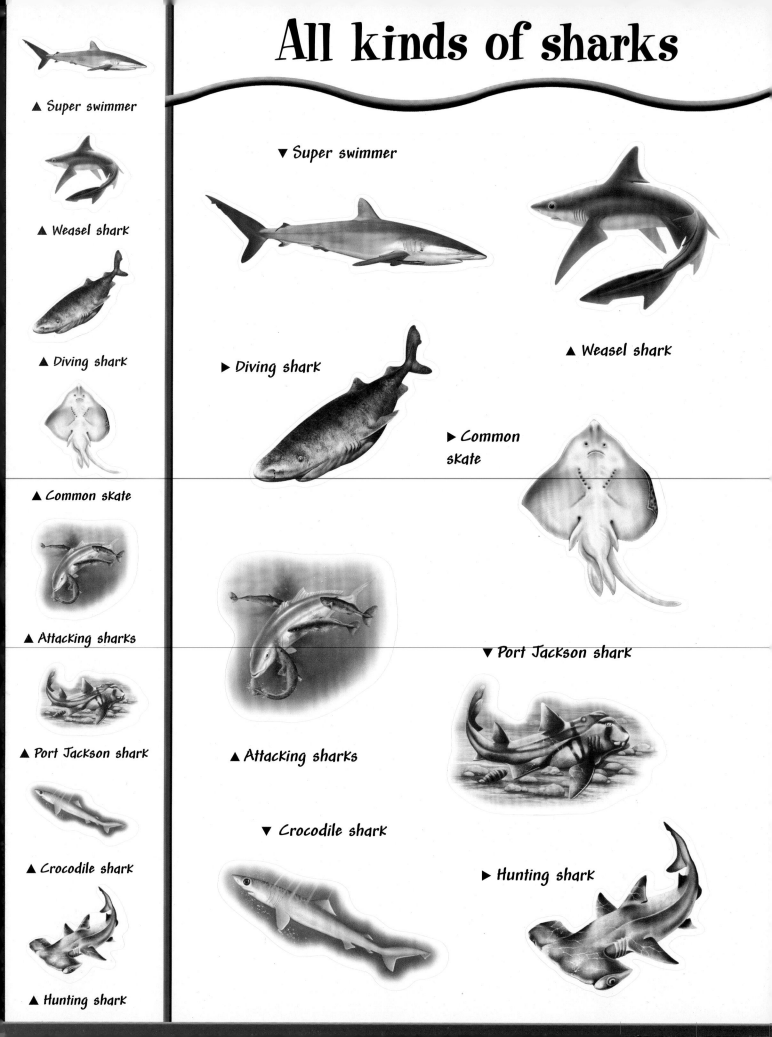

All kinds of sharks

▲ Super swimmer

▲ Weasel shark

▲ Diving shark

▲ Common skate

▲ Attacking sharks

▲ Port Jackson shark

▲ Crocodile shark

▲ Hunting shark

▼ Super swimmer

► Diving shark

▲ Weasel shark

► Common skate

▲ Attacking sharks

▼ Port Jackson shark

▼ Crocodile shark

► Hunting shark

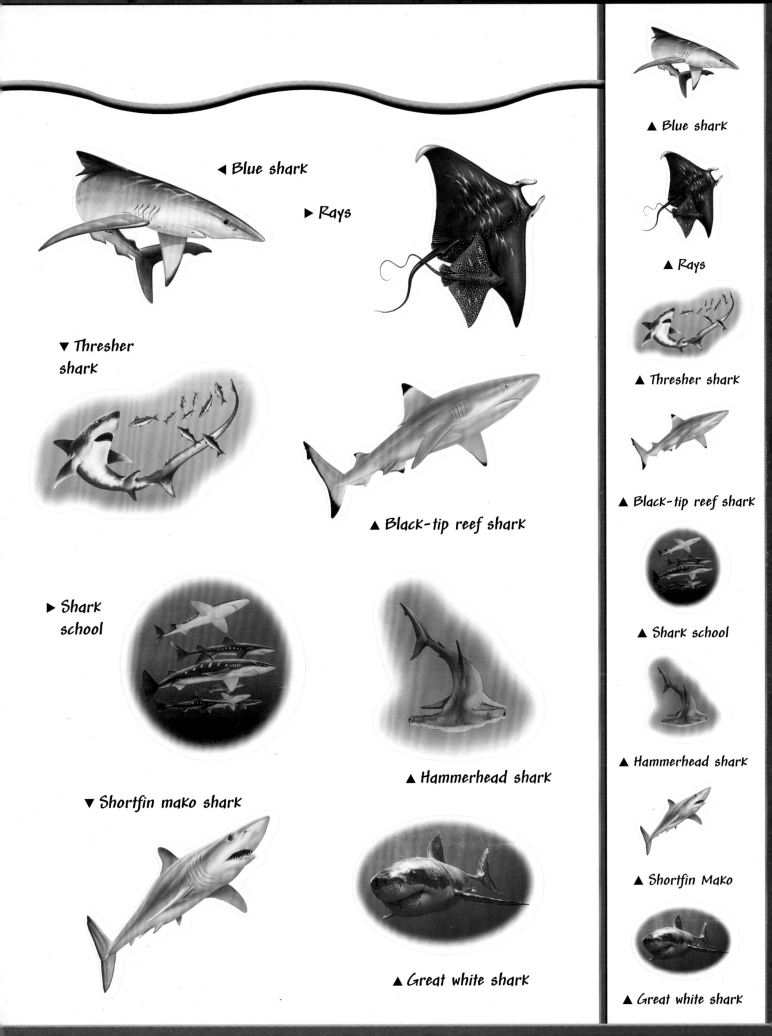

◀ Blue shark

▶ Rays

▼ Thresher shark

▲ Black-tip reef shark

▶ Shark school

▲ Hammerhead shark

▼ Shortfin mako shark

▲ Great white shark

All kinds of sharks

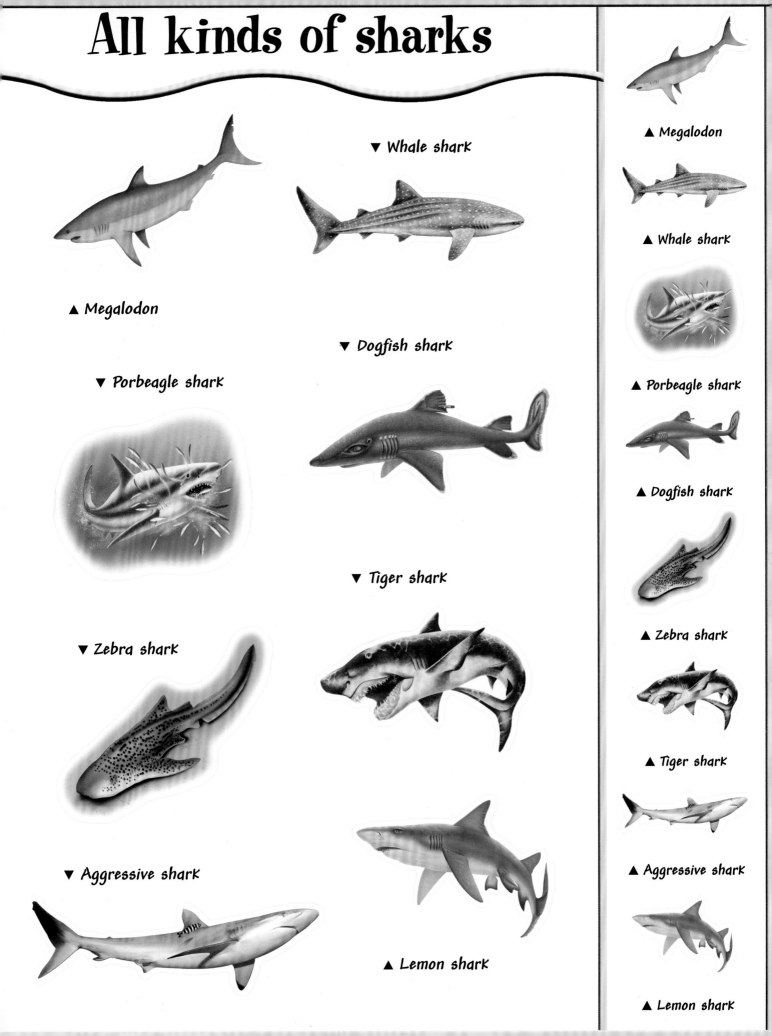

▼ Whale shark

▲ Megalodon

▼ Dogfish shark

▼ Porbeagle shark

▼ Tiger shark

▼ Zebra shark

▼ Aggressive shark

▲ Lemon shark

▲ Megalodon

▲ Whale shark

▲ Porbeagle shark

▲ Dogfish shark

▲ Zebra shark

▲ Tiger shark

▲ Aggressive shark

▲ Lemon shark

Giant shark!

Most sharks are big. The whale shark is a giant – it grows to more than 15 metres long and can weigh over 20 tonnes! It is the world's biggest fish, but is not a fierce hunter.

A whale shark swims with its mouth open, filtering small animals such as fish and krill from the water with its special comblike gills. Like all sharks, it cannot chew – it just swallows its food whole!

The whale shark has a spotty back and pale underside.

Shark race for two!

You will need:

• tissue paper • scissors • newspapers • plates

1. Cut out two tissue-paper sharks. Each one should be about 30 centimetres long.

2. Lie the sharks flat on their backs. Place two plates about 3 metres away on the other side of the room.

3. Hit the ground just behind the shark with a rolled-up newspaper to make it move. The shark that lands on the plate first is the winner.

Shark time

▶ Rays
Filter feeders, like the basking and whale shark – rays suck in seawater and filter tiny plankton out of it

▶ Great white shark
Fish, seals and sealions are the favourite foods of great whites

▶ Shortfin mako shark
Recorded swimming at over 30 kilometres per hour, this is the fastest shark

▶ Hammerhead shark
These are some of the smartest sharks – they are fast, fierce hunters

▼ Thresher shark
The thresher shark sweeps its enormous tail from side to side to stun small fish before eating them

◀ Shark school
Sharks sometimes swim in schools of hundreds or even thousands

▶ Blue shark
This shark does not normally attack humans, but it has been reported to attack the survivors of sunken ships

▲ Black-tip reef shark
These sharks have black marks on the tips of each of their fins

KEY:

 How sharks live

 Extraordinary sharks

 Shark relatives

 Fierce sharks

► Zebra shark
When young, zebra sharks have dark and light stripes – as adults the stripes separate into blotches

► Megalodon
Probably the biggest shark ever, Megalodon lived millions of years ago – it may have been very similar to a great white shark

▼ Aggressive shark
An upward-pointed snout, arched back and downward-pointed fins means this shark is in a bad mood and ready to attack

▼ Whale shark
The largest shark in the world, the whale shark can be up to 12 metres long!

▼ Lemon shark
Stings from stingrays have been found embedded in the mouths of lemon sharks

► Porbeagle shark
The porbeagle can travel long distances, following schools of fish around the ocean

► Dogfish shark
There are around 80 shark species that make up the huge dogfish family

▲ Tiger shark
Tiger sharks have even been seen eating other tiger sharks!

A reindeer was once found inside a dead Greenland shark's stomach!

Biggest and best

Mako sharks can leap 6 metres clear of the water's surface.

There is a better chance of winning the lottery than being attacked by a shark.

In 1758 it was reported that a sailor had been swallowed whole by a shark, it is said that the shark was made to throw up and the man was recovered unharmed!

Read more about some record-breaking sharks

• The longest shark in the sea is the whale shark – it can grow up to 15 metres long. That is more than four times bigger than the average human!

• Megalodon lived over 2 million years ago. Scientists believe that its mouth was over 2 metres wide. That's big enough to eat several people in one go!

• The largest great white shark ever caught weighed a staggering 4.5 tonnes – that is only just lighter than a fully grown elephant!

Q: What do you get from a fierce shark?
A: As far away as possible!

Shark facts

Discover some fascinating facts about sharks

• A shark can have as many as 300 teeth at one time. If a tooth is damaged, it is quickly replaced with a new one. In a lifetime sharks can use about 20,000 teeth!

• Baby sharks are called pups. They can look after themselves as soon as they are born. Sometimes they have a small yolk sac that supplies nutrients until the young shark starts to eat properly.

• Sharks' skeletons are not made of bone, but of a material called cartilage, which is like rubber. This means that sharks are very flexible and they can twist and turn easily in the water.

Some shark scientists believe that spiny dogfish can live for up to 100 years!

A lemon shark has been recorded swimming at 32 kilometres per hour. The shortfin mako is thought to swim even faster.

When a shark is turned onto its back it goes limp and sleepy. This helps scientists to study them.

Q: What is yellow and dangerous?
A: Shark-infested custard!

Fun facts

Sharks do not chew their food, they swallow chunks whole!

Great white sharks can go for 3 whole months without eating.

Sharks will often take a bite of something to see if they like the taste. If they don't, they spit it back out!

Test your memory!

How much can you remember from your sharks sticker activity book? Find out below!

1. How many species are in the dogfish family: 80, 800 or 8000?
2. Which is the biggest shark ever: the megamouth, Megalodon or the mako shark?
3. Does the zebra shark have stripes when it is young?
4. What do saw sharks use their saws for?
5. Which is the fastest shark?
6. Sharks are fish: true or false?
7. What will happen to a shark if it stops swimming: will it change colour, sink or float?
8. Do sharks usually go hunting during the day or the night?
9. Where do black-tip reef sharks have their black markings?
10. How many years do some scientists believe a dogfish can live: 30, 70 or 100?

Q: What is a shark's favourite game?
A: Swallow the leader!

11. What can sharks not do: chew their food, swim or smell?
12. All sharks are blind: true or false?
13. Which of the following does the great white shark not like to eat: fish, vegetables or seals?
14. How wide is the megamouth's mouth?
15. Do sharks have fur, scales or feathers?
16. Where do Greenland sharks live?
17. What other animals are frilled sharks often mistaken for?
18. The crocodile shark has eyes that take up almost half of its head: true or false?
19. How many teeth can sharks have at once?
20. Does the Port Jackson shark give birth to live young?

Answers:

1. 80 2. Megalodon 3. No – spots 4. Digging up prey from the seabed 5. Shortfin mako 6. True 7. Sink 8. The night 9. On the tips of their fins 10. 100 11. Chew their food 12. False 13. Vegetables 14. One metre wide 15. Scales 16. The North Atlantic Ocean 17. Eels or sea snakes 18. True 19. 300 20. No – they lay eggs

Some sharks can smell small amounts of blood in the water from hundreds of metres away.

A blue shark was tagged in waters around New York. Sixteen months later it was recaptured in Brazilian waters, over 6000 kilometres away!

If a shark stops swimming it will slowly sink to the bottom of the ocean!

Q: Why didn't the shark bite the clown?
A: Because he tasted funny!

www.animalplanet.co.uk

Animal Planet is all things animal.

Like an animal itself, Animal Planet is gripping, instinctual, exciting and alive. Animal Planet tells real-life stories with animals in the lead roles. You can see the personality of each animal shine through, reminding us how much we have in common with those that share our planet.

10 STICKER FUN BOOKS TO COLLECT

Amazing website packed with pictures!

yourdiscovery.com/web/animalplanet

Invite the natural world into your home with Animal Planet – bringing you closer to the animals that you love.

Fantastic magazine for hours of fun!

animalplanetmagazine.co.uk

Animal Planet is the perfect magazine for boys and girls who are interested in learning more about our fascinating planet and the mesmerising animals of the land and sea.

Crammed with fun facts, breathtaking animals and cool projects, Animal Planet encourages children to let their imagination lead the way and release the explorer within!